Social Media Strategy

70 Social Media Strategies to Boost Your Business

By Lancaster Collins

Pogo Book Publishing

Copyright © 2013 Pogo Book Publishing
All rights reserved.
ISBN: 978-1494720254
ISBN-13: 1494720256

TABLE OF CONTENTS

INTRODUCTION

Social Media Marketing: A Brief Overview

Top Facebook Marketing Strategy

TOP TWITTER MARKETING strategy

TOP GOOGLE+ MARKETING strategy

TOP LinkedIn MARKETING strategy

Unleashing The Power Of IMAGEs In INSTAGRAM

TOP Pinterest MARKETING STRATEGY

YouTubE AND unleashing THE POWER OF VIDEO

CONCLUSION

INTRODUCTION

Social media marketing becomes more and more important nowadays. Why we say that? Let us understand the current phenomenon of business industry first.

Businesses are now getting more and more virtual when compared to the conventional ways of selling things. The advancement of technology is the key of this big change. Many people prefer to shop online than visiting shop themselves.

Therefore, there are increasing number of online businesses popped out. This indicates that the level of competition is also getting tougher as time goes by.

All the business owners wish to find ways to get noticed, build their online brand, attract customers and increase their sales. That is why social media comes to its place.

By using social media, which is now an ongoing trend when it comes to online marketing strategy, the business owner will have that much needed leverage to stay in this competitive game and flourish in the online world.

Although there are several online marketing strategies that can be used by business owners nowadays such as blogging for business, press releasing and so on, the social media strategy still remain as the most effective way of marketing as it creates the largest buzz to the world. Small sized businesses and large scale corporations are using this to promote their products and services.

Its popularity as a tool used to boost one's online marketing strategy is undeniable. If you are in search of an effective and affordable means of marketing your company, then social media is definitely what you are looking for.

You will be provided with the 70 proven strategies to boost your online business by using social media. These strategies are divided and categorized according to the type of platform to be used.

It's up to you to choose which social media platform is best for your business or you can use them all. You will notice that you will be reaping the benefits of your labor in no time.

Social Media Marketing: A Brief Overview

In order to reach out to a wider target audience, we have to use the social media sites that consist of a lot of members all over the world. We have chosen the top 7 famous social media platforms for this book. Each of them have millions of active members that might be your potential clients.

If you are able to include all of these social media platforms as part of your online marketing strategy, I'm sure this will be a powerful boost for your business.

Social media marketing is referred to the process of promoting or marketing your company as well as the products and services which you are offering by using the social media.

This is also an effective way of gaining better company branding. This is considered as one of the most affordable online marketing strategy. It involves content, photo and video sharing for the purposes of increasing web traffic, online presence and sales.

There are few things which the business owner can do with social media. Each of these things will surely provide the business owner some benefits as following:

- Better company branding
- Increase the exposure about your products and services to the world
- Interact, socialize, engage and build a stronger relationship with your customers
- Getting new customers while retaining existing ones
- Better customer support can be provided

There are many reasons why you should apply the social media strategies. Many business owners choose to use social media to establish the identity and brand of their company.

With social media, the business owners can create the buzz for their business and attract more new customers. The exposure for the products and services will increase by engaging with others through social media.

Social media is a good way of marketing because of its viral effect. Most of the social media sites have a share button which means that one person can help us to share out the information. If they do so, our business will have the potential to go viral. This definitely will help our business to gain more exposure once they share your posts to their friends and families.

In addition, people tend to spend more time on social media sites nowadays. They prefer to leave feedbacks and comments on social media sites then sending email or calling. You also get to know what other people are saying about your company, products and services. With these feedbacks, you will be given the opportunity to improve your products and make it more well fitted to the needs of your customers. Also, you will be able to answer the queries of your customers in a professional, timely and interactive manner.

Furthermore, your website will also have higher SEO ranking by applying these social media strategies. Google is now paying more attention to websites which has a good social media reputation and standing. The social signals are important for Google to know how popular your business is.

Top Facebook Marketing Strategy

As all of us know, Facebook is the most popular social media site for these few years. With its huge list of members, we will definitely have the tremendous online exposure that we have always wanted to gain from it. It is easy for us to reach out to the audiences by having a Facebook business page with tons of useful contents.

Tip #1 – Get Facebook Users to Like or Share your Page

Having a Facebook business page is the first step for Facebook Marketing strategy. You must invite as much Facebook users to like or share your page. In order to do so, you must have a lot of valuable and interesting content on your Facebook page. Content is always the most important thing for the Facebook users to consider whether want to like or share your page. Therefore, create only good content and start to invite others to like and share your page. You will definitely get the exposure that you want.

Tip #2 - Post Something that Engaging the Everyone

When you are posting something on your Facebook page, you have to make sure that it is informative and relevant to what your company is actually offering. You have to topic-specific on what you post on your page. You can write about a specific current event, articles, pictures or videos which can easily be tied to your business. Remember to ask people to leave some comments or feedback on what you post to drive the engagement.

Tip #3 – Use Different Types of Content

The good thing for Facebook is that you can post any type of content that you like. You can use plain text, add in a couple of photos or even use videos with caption. Take advantage of the features offered by this social media site and make the most out of it. Obviously, video is the most engaging and potentially goes viral in Facebook.

Tip #4 – Utilize Facebook Ads

Alternatively, you may use Facebook Ads. You can find the ads on the sidebar of Facebook. You can utilize this to drive more traffic to your own Facebook Business page or to your business website. An ad would contain a featured image, a brief description, a call-to-action and a link which you can use to direct the viewers to your fan page or to your main site. However, you might need to spend some money for that. It can be Pay-Per-Click or Pay-Per-Impression.

Tip #5 - Immediate Response

Immediate response is one of the key success for a Facebook page. It is very important that you pay attention to your audiences especially those who have comments or questions about your content on Facebook. Social media has to be used for interacting with audiences. Therefore, replying promptly to their concerns should be on top of your priority. Doing this would let your audiences know that you treat their feedback and comment seriously. If you fail to do this, you can expect your fan page to drastically weaken in an instant.

Tip #6 – Update Your Page Regularly

In contrast to the conventional way of media marketing, using an online social media requires you to provide regular posts with fresh and valuable content. Facebook users would appreciate business pages that are capable of providing them with new and informative content on a regular basis. Just imagine if they see a notification update from your Facebook page every time they open their Facebook page, I'm sure this will increase the exposure exponentially.

Tip #7 - Be Creative and Innovative

When managing your business fan page, you really have to be as creative and innovative as possible. You don't want to be considered as boring by your audiences. Be creative. Be innovative. Be funny. You can make each and every post you share as enjoyable as possible. Although the main purpose of the content is to promote your products and services, you may it interesting and exciting. This will build up a better interaction with your audiences therefore, increasing your online presence and the public's awareness of your brand.

Tip #8 – Put Relevant Business Apps to Your Page

It is also important that you add the necessary applications to your Facebook business page. This will greatly help in making sure that your audiences will have a good user experience when browsing your page. This is just an extra point for a good Facebook page. We want to get as much advantage if compare to other Facebook pages.

Tip #9 – Organize Facebook Contest

Organizing an interesting contest on your Facebook page will definitely boost up the engagement among the users on your page. Almost all individuals love to participate in contests. The thrill and the excitement it gives are amazing. There are several third party applications which can help you out with this. Think of an interesting type of contest and give it a go. The prizes will always be your products and services. This is a good marketing strategy for you.

Tip #10 – Monitoring and Tracking Your Marketing Effort

It is important for you to monitor and track the effectiveness of your marketing effort via Facebook. Without monitoring it, you will not know what to improve and what is the best effort that you have made on your Facebook page. In every marketing strategy, you have to find out if what you have actually implemented is providing you with the results which you are expecting. If you are using the Facebook ads, you will get the analytic stat on your dashboard. The Facebook page will have its own tracking statistic too. Remember to monitor and track according to the statistic especially the user behavior.

Remember, social media strategies require time and a lot of effort so do not expect to see tremendous changes in a just a couple of days. Give it time and be genuinely enthusiastic and committed with what you are doing and you will surely gain the benefits.

Top Twitter Marketing Strategy

Twitter is another big social media guy that still maintains it popularity for quite a long time. It offers a micro blogging service which is also one of the most effective social media platform used for online marketing. It allows its users to post a very short description of 140 characters. We can use this platform to market our products and services effectively too.

Tip #11 – Develop a Proper Twitter Account with Business Brand

Share the story of your business through your twitter account. This will certainly influence the response of other people to you. And, by setting up your account properly, your followers will be able to identify your business brand apart from your competitors. The name and the image that you choose must be consistent with your other profiles which have been set up on a different medium and it should also be easily associated with your company's identity.

Tip #12 – Acquire Followers Strategically

The most important part of Twitter marketing strategy is to have a huge list of followers for your account. You must design an effective strategy to acquire more followers. When startup, it is recommended to follow the followers from other Twitter accounts which are in the same niche of your business. Most of the time, people will follow you back if you have good contents posting on your Twitter account. Go slow when doing this since Twitter has rigid guidelines when it comes to excessive following and they suspend accounts once they find it as suspicious.

Tip #13 – Share Interesting Tweets

Similar to Facebook marketing strategy, the contents that you post on your Twitter account plays a vital role on your marketing effort. So, just post some interesting tweets related to your business products and services which have the potential to be retweeted by others. With twitter, users are provided an easier way to share topics which they find interesting. This is one of the main reasons why so many individuals love this social media site. Make use of the 140 character description properly by creating a catchy statement which would draw in the interest of your followers.

Tip #14 – Only Follow those Related to Your Business

You must choose the people that you want to follow wisely because once you do, you will be reading whatever posts they share. This is important to find out what your audiences are concerning. You can follow your clients, contractors, suppliers and other individuals within your professional network.

Tip #15 – Gather Market Info

Many people do not aware that Twitter actually is a good place to gather market information. You can use Twitter to find what your target clients need and interested. By looking at what your audiences tweet and share about, you will understand more on them. By doing this, you can easily find the sweet pot of all audiences so that you can provide a solution to their problems or answer their questions and you will be considered as worth following by other members.

Tip #16 – Treat Every Single Tweet Seriously

Do not tweet something unrelated to your business on your Twitter account. You have to treat every single tweet seriously. It will significantly affect your business credibility. Learn how to post in Twitter. This aspect is very important knowing for a fact that you are only allowed to have a micro blog which is 140 characters long. Try out different ways of writing the post before actually posting it. Create interesting posts which will draw in other users to actually read what you have just posted.

Tip #17 – Link Up with Other Platforms

Twitter has a feature for you to link up your account with Facebook. This will greatly help your social marketing effort. And, it is very important to connect your twitter account to your actual business website. This social networking site offers an option wherein you can simply add your website to your twitter account. You can also make use of their widget which will allow you to share your tweet timeline to your business website. By doing so, your website visitors will be able to view your actual conversations in twitter. It's like hitting two birds with one stone. Lastly, add a twitter button to your site so that your website visitors can share the content of your website to their twitter account.

Tip #18 – Utilize the Image

Many people do not aware that Twitter also allows photo sharing. You can post images related to your business or some important events which took place in your company. Images are far more eye-capturing than plain texts. So, use it properly.

Tip #19 – Monitoring and Tracking

Similar to Facebook marketing, we have to monitor and track the marketing effectiveness on Twitter too. It is a must on every marketing process to find out the efficiency of the implemented plan. Through this, you will be able to make the needed improvements so that you will be able to hit your desired targets. Understanding your audiences' behavior is an essential element to boost your business in long run.

Tip #20 – Market Your Twitter

Finally, you may also promote your Twitter account on Facebook and your website. Some of the audiences might prefer to use Twitter than Facebook. By doing so, you allow the audiences to choose their preference while following business updates and share.

Top Google+ Marketing Strategy

Many people have overlooked the potential of Google+ as a powerful marketing tool for their business. In fact, it is as powerful as Facebook marketing and Twitter marketing if we utilize it in a correct way. Once you master the right techniques of using this platform, you will not only increase your online visibility, web traffic and sales but you also get to have an excellent Google search engine positioning.

Tip #21 – Google Account Profile Creation

Creating Google account profile is important for your online marketing effort. As we all know, Google offers a lot of useful marketing tools such as Google Place, Google Authorship and so on which are good for our business. The fact is, all of these services will link to your Google Account Profile including Google+. So, you really need to take your time when creating one for your business. You also have to make sure that you have thought about your introduction. Make it stand out above all the others so that other users will add you to their circles. Put some links on your profile page such as Facebook page and Twitter account. You want to make sure that your profile are filled with all your business information.

Tip #22 – Stunning Company Logo

Company logo is the first thing that people will see from your Google Profile. Only upload the high resolution company logo to your profile. It is important to grab the attention and build up the brand for your business.

Tip #23 – Make Your Profile Searchable

When setting up your account in Google+, you have to be sure that you put a check mark on the option where in it would allow others to find your profile. This is very important since being searchable in search engines would give you better chances of your profile in being indexed.

Tip #24 – Organize Your Google+ Circles

Similar to Twitter, you will be able to categorize the people that you interact with accordingly. These categories can be by profession, business, personal, friends, acquaintances and many more. You can even create one for your target customers. This offers better organization which can be very useful for your business.

Tip #25 – Interaction and Connection

The heart of social media lies within interaction and connection with other people. Similar to other social media platforms, you have to make sure that you connect and interact with others in Google+. It is never enough to just create a profile and just hope things will work out. It needs you as the driving force to make your social media strategy to work. Yes, this can be time consuming but the results are definitely worth all your hard work and patience.

Tip #26 – Hash tags

Many people do not aware of the feature of hash tags on Google+. Like Facebook and twitter, Google+ also has their hash tags. Make use of it and benefit from it. By using these, you can access the users who are following those hash tags which you used on your posts. This is the best way to see the audiences' behavior too.

Tip #27 – Post Good Content

Content is always to king when talking about social media engagement and marketing. Post a good content on your Google+ and engage with your audiences. You can do this by posting images, texts, videos, relevant links and many more. You can even tag other people just like the other social networking sites. Remember, do not overdo this. It can be considered as spamming. You do not want to drive people away from your business by spamming.

Tip #28 – Utilize Google+ Hangouts

The Google+ Hangouts is another great feature from Google too. This feature allows you to hold conferences or meetings with people in your circles. It works the same as Skype. You can even use this feature to stream live to a big number of audiences. Maximize the utility of the Google+ Hangouts will definitely boost your business to the next level.

Tip #29 – Update Consistently

Post fresh content and being active in Google+ is just as important as organizing a business event. People do not like to follow a page that is inactive. So, keep your Google+ fresh so that people know that you are care about your business.

Tip #30 – Create Uniqueness

Make your Google+ page as unique as possible. This can be done by creating unique content at all times. This is one key aspect that you should apply to your online marketing strategy when creating posts not only for your Google+ page but to all other sites that you have. Audiences want to read a content which is not only informative but is unique as well. If your write ups are similar to what your competitors have, then you are doing it the wrong way. You will end up losing followers and all your efforts will be gone to waste.

Top LinkedIn Marketing Strategy

LinkedIn is another big social media site right now. It is slightly different with other social media platforms that we talked about previously. It is a place for people to share their expertise, their interests, their specialties and so on. It is just like a place for people to post their resumes online. Therefore, it is not only good for business, it can be utilized as a self-promoting tool for all the individuals. You can find new customers, enhance your business relationships and connect with other individuals who share the same interests as you do. However, you have to make sure that you employ the right strategy when using this platform so that you will be able to make the most out of it.

Tip #31 – Create a Client Focused Profile

Since LinkedIn has so many fields allotted for your personal, business or employment background, make sure that you do not end up making a resume instead of an interesting business profile. Design your profile and focus to your target clients. Write a brief and easy-to-understand description which would let the audiences know what your company is all about, what benefits will they gain if they choose your products and services as well as inform them why your company is the best. Make a great start by creating a profile which will have a great impact and leave a good impression.

Tip #32 – Utilize the Search Feature

One good feature of LinkedIn is the search feature. You can find new clients by making use the search feature. So, use it intelligently and wisely. You will find a lot of potential customers from there. You can also use this feature in finding the profiles that related to your business and build up the possible collaboration relationship too.

Tip #33 – Build Good Deep Connections

Only build a good connections. So, choose wisely when you connect with others. You need to make connections to those whom you think you can create or develop a great business relationship. Your connections must be productive and efficient. The deeper the connections you have with your network the better.

Tip #34 – Productive Recommendations

People can recommend you some good profiles as well as receiving recommendations from you. Although you cannot beg for recommendations from others, you can always give a recommendation to a person or business which you have worked with. People tend to do the same once you do this. They will usually give you a good recommendations too. You can also use this same process with endorsements. Great endorsements and recommendations mean making a better impression to your target clients.

Tip #35 – Connect with Targeted Groups

All the members of each group in LinkedIn share the same interests. You might need to connect with those groups that are closely related to your products and services. You can monitor those groups to see the current trend and concern in your niche by looking and the events and discussions in the group. You can build your credibility through these groups and boost up the exposure of your business significantly.

Tip #36 – Quality Status Updates

Only post the quality status updates on your LinkedIn. Make sure that it is interesting and exciting. This is a good way to constantly remind your clients about what you do about your business. You can use it as an advertising and marketing strategy for your new products or services too. But remember, hard selling doesn't work in social media marketing. Try to make it as interesting as possible.

Tip #37 – Check Others' Updates Frequently

You might find some interesting and great opportunities from others' updates too. So, do check out others' status updates frequently. If you find some potential opportunity, you may contact them and discuss more about how both of you can take advantage from what you can offer. Once you get a hold of the person of interest, initiate a polite conversation and start establishing a good business relationship. And, if you find some interesting status updates from others, you may also learn from it so that you can post something great for others in your account too. This is a great way of learning.

Tip #38 – Link Up with Other Social Media Platforms

As its name suggested, LinkedIn is great to link up people as well as your social profiles too. This is the place that you can share all your social profiles on one page so that people can easily follow you on different social platforms. This is a great way for you to build up the credibility for your business as well as yourself. You will certainly deliver a good impression to the audiences when seeing all of your social profiles on LinkedIn.

Tip #39 – Utilize the Applications

Similar to other social media sites, LinkedIn allows you to add some applications to your account. These apps will help you market your business effectively. Try to locate some good applications that suitable for your business marketing strategy and add it to your LinkedIn account.

Tip #40 – Optimize Your Profile

Do not forget to optimize your profile so that it is searchable by others. It is important to allow other potential customers to be able to find you as well as your business. You don't want to miss a business opportunity because of that. So, put some relevant information on your profile strategically.

Unleashing the Power of Images in Instagram

The fact is, Instagram has been overlooked to be a marketing tool for business. It is more than just a photo sharing community. If we know the way to utilize it to market our business, it will definitely bring our business to the next level. Let us find out how to do it effectively.

Tip #41 – Use Your Business Name

Remember to use your business name as your Instagram username. This is important for your business branding as well as your identity. People can easily recognize your business based on your Instagram username.

Tip #42 – Informative and Client Focused Profile

Similar to other social platforms, your profile is where everything begins. Be as comprehensive as possible when making your profile. You can introduce your company's values and objectives. Try to make it as simple as possible without compromising your business identity and what you can offer to the clients. Send the right message by properly creating your Instagram profile.

Tip #43 – Look for Your Target Audiences

Instagram's search feature is good for you to locate target audiences who are looking for the products and services that you are offering. And, seldom people know that actually we can utilize the hash tags on Instagram to find the potential audiences too. By locating your target audiences, you have to analyze their interactions in Instagram as well as finding out their main concern and ultimately find the sweet spot that can solve their problems. Stay connect with your target audiences and engage with them.

Tip #44 – Share Informative Images

Images is one of the most capturing contents in social networking. A good image has the potential to go viral. So, make sure that you share some interesting and informative images which related to your business to millions of audiences in the top photo sharing community in the world. Share the images that tell story about your products and services. Conventional advertising posters will not work for this purpose. So, make sure you choose your images wisely.

Tip #45 – Create or Capture the Images Yourself

One diligent way to utilize Instagram as an effective marketing tool for your business is to create the images yourself. You can also capture some good images yourself. This will definitely create the uniqueness to your Instagram account and ultimately build up the brand of your business. Of course, you have to make sure that the pictures you posts are all amazing. You therefore, have to make sure that you have somebody who knows how to take great pictures or learn how to do it yourself. The success of your strategy implemented in Instagram, greatly lies on the photos which you will be sharing. Learn the various techniques of taking great pictures.

Tip #46 – Behind the Scenes Photos

One great way of connecting to your customers as well as allowing them to get to know you better is by posting photos of things that is happening within your company. This is a great way to build up the relationship between your business with the audiences. You can post shots during an event preparation or perhaps during an office eat out. You can take candid shots too. Doing this, will allow your customers have an inside view of what is happening with your company.

Tip #47 – Create a Stunning Products Gallery

You may want to use the Instagram to create a stunning products gallery that will grab attention and deliver message. Remember to feature your best selling product so that people will notice it straight away by looking at your products gallery. Post the best shots as possible to attract the attention of your potential targets. You don't want to put up some low quality images of your products to ruin the audiences' impression on it. Remember! Product images play a vital for the customers to decide whether want to buy it or not. So, make it as attractive as possible.

Tip #48 – Showcase Your Team

People love to buy from merchants that look legit and trustworthy. One way you can increase the confidence of audiences to our business is to showcase the image of your team. This will all the audiences to know the individuals who are responsible for the great company that you have. Your employees too would love this. Add up a short description about each employee and you are good to go.

Tip #49 – Engage with Your Audiences

Again, engagement is essential for Instagram marketing too. You have to make sure that you engage with your audiences frequently. You can leave comment and share other individual's photos occasionally to build up the relationship. Simply posting your photos will not guarantee that you will have tons of followers right away. You have to engage with other users as much as you can and also make sure that your comments are relevant and insightful.

Tip #50 – Be Creative and Innovative

Try to be creative and innovative when sharing images in Instagram. There are many software or applications that allow you to make or edit your images so that they looks more attractive and desirable. Utilize those tools so that you images can stand up from the crowd to grab attention!

Top Pinterest Marketing Strategy

Pinterest is one of the fast-growing social networking sites too. Its concept is simple. Just pin something interesting on your board and share with others. This is a good platform especially for businesses which concentrates on various types of products. It is a very effective medium if you wish to promote your products on a wider target market with the use of photos! Although it is new compared to other social media platforms, it is one of the most used marketing platforms for business.

Tip #51 – Build a Business Account

Setting up a business account on Pinterest is a great way to build up the credibility and identity for your business. It can help to boost up the exposure for your products and services too. So, spend some time to create your business account with an informative profile on it.

Tip #52 – Fully Utilized the Tools

There are a lot of useful tools for you to use in Pinterest. You might want to fully utilized them for your business. This can incredibly increase the exposure of your products and services to the audiences. Some of the tools such PicMonkey, PinAlert and so on are really useful for your marketing effort.

Tip #53 – Monitoring and Tracking

Similarly to other social platforms, you must monitor and track the efficiency of your marketing effort in Pinterest. There are some nice tools that can help you to do so such as Piqora and some other tools that can do the same job. Make sure you check on them regularly to understand what you need to improve and what you should not do while doing business marketing on Pinterest.

Tip #54 – Make Sure Your Pinterest Site is Pinnable

Please do make sure that your Pinterest site is pinnable so that people can easily share your site and spread to others easily. You want to make your Pinterest site as interesting as possible so that people are interested on sharing your site.

Tip #55 – Choose Product Pins

In fact, there are three types o pins that can be used in Pinterest. Since you are using it for your products marketing and promotion, it is always recommended to choose product pins. One of the great things by doing so is the product pins include the price tag. For who repins your product pins will be notified if there is any update on the price in the future.

Tip #56 – Target Your Potential Audiences

Please do not get mad as I keep repeating this again and again in each and of the social platform marketing strategy. This is one of the key success for social media marketing for your business. You have to target your potential audiences wisely so that your marketing effort is really worthwhile.

Tip #57 – Organize Events or Contests

In order to boost up the engagement with your audiences, organizing events and contests are highly recommended. Through the events or contests, your audiences will know more about your business and will potentially become your customers in a long run.

Tip #58 – Pin Some Educational Pieces

If you are able to pin some educational pieces and help your audiences, this will definitely boost up the popularity and credibility for your Pinterest site. Please don't bore your audiences with constant products promotion pins only. People do not like to be advertised often. Try to find some educational information and pin them on your site.

Tip #59 – Engage With Others

You also have to comment, like and re-pinning the pins of others. Social media means you have to connect to the other members of the community. This applies to all platforms and not just in Pinterest.

Tip #60 – Monitor your Competitors

Sometimes, it is good to see what your competitors have done for their marketing effort. You may use Pinterest to do so. Try to monitor what your competitors have pinned and shared in their Pinterest site. If it is good, you may employ it for yourself. But, please do not copy exactly on what it is. Build up some uniqueness while absorbing their good things. This will definitely help you to improve your marketing strategy in a long run.

YouTube and Unleashing The Power of Video

YouTube has been known as the first and the best video sharing community in the world. It becomes more and more popular after the acquisition of Google. Google has transformed YouTube to become another good social media which is good for business marketing. The reason why I put this as the last social platform in this book is because it provides the most visual experience to the audiences which is extremely useful for us. It can be the most effective social media strategy if we know how to use it.

Tip #61 – Build Your Business Channel

Building a channel for your business on YouTube is the first step that you need to do for YouTube marketing. There are many research showed that a YouTube channel actually gives more opportunities than uploading videos without any channel. A channel itself can be as much informative as your video. You can easily organize your videos via the channel so that your audience can easily follow them too. A channel will enable you to promote all your videos at once rather than promoting them one by one. You just need to promote your channel to your audiences and they can easily watch all of the videos under the same channel.

Tip #62 – Publish Only Captivating Videos

The content of the videos that you publish on YouTube is the key element for YouTube marketing. You want to make sure that you only publish some captivating videos which have the potential to reach millions of views on YouTube and creating a buzz in other social platforms. We can call those videos as viral videos. Just imagine if you have a viral video that being shared across all the social platforms and generated millions of views, I'm sure you will be stunned to see how big the effect on boosting up your business. Please do not publish some low quality videos that just filled up with texts and bring zero value to the audiences. It will definitely affect your business reputation as well as the credibility. You don't want to ruin all your marketing effort just because of a low quality video. Therefore, make sure that your video delivers good message and even solution to the audiences.

Tip #63 – Emphasize on People's Needs

A viral video for business marketing purpose has to be valuable to the audiences. You have to emphasize on people's needs in your video but not just hard selling your products or services. If your video is informative and helpful to the audiences, it will definitely gain the audiences' trust and confidence towards your business. People will tend to share something that is useful to everyone. Remember! Clicking on the "Share" button is far more easier than cracking the nuts shell. If your video appears to be valuable, people won't mind to share it to others.

Tip #64 – Outsource Your Video Production

Making a video these days isn't rocket science. You may choose to generate the video yourself or just outsource to others to produce for you. The truth is, the cost for making high quality videos have gone down especially when high definition cameras are quite easy to obtain as well as video editing software. You can easily outsource the video production project to others and focus on how to market it to your targeted audiences. A short video with 4 to 5 minutes is sufficient for your YouTube marketing. Do not create a long duration video which might potentially bore your audiences.

Tip #65 – Optimize Your Video Listing

As we all know, many businesses have started to use video as their main marketing tool. There are tons of videos uploaded to YouTube for every single minute. So, it is important for you to fully optimized your video listing so that it is discoverable by the audiences. A good combination of title, description, and tags is the best way to optimize the video. However, do not spam the keywords on your description as Google might remove your video or even ban your account by doing that.

Tip #66 – Check out the Comments and Feedback

One of the mistakes that most marketers have done is to ignore the comments and feedback for the videos. They chose to delete the bad comments or feedback without trying to improve the video. This does not help at all. In contrast, we should treat the comments and feedback as a valuable information for us to improve our video production. Try to engage with the audiences by replying to the comments and feedback.

Tip #67 – Build Subscribers List

One of the best features that YouTube has is the subscribing feature. People can subscribe to the channel that they like so that they will be informed when there is update on that particular channel. Hence, creating an informative and helpful channel is important for people to subscribe to your YouTube channel. You will want to have a big number of subscribers for you channel so that you can market your products or services effectively.

Tip #68 – Share On Other Social Sites

You may use the videos that you have published on YouTube as the content for your regular updates on other social sites too. So, you will be the first person to share your video to the audiences. Videos appear to be a high value content for social media sharing. So, use it diligently and creatively.

Tip #69 – Call to Action

These annotations will appear in your video as specified. It may appear anytime you wish but preferably at the end of the video or when announcing something important. CTA's or call to action provides more reasons to get in touch with your video or brand. You could offer instructional guides, discount coupons, or even offer a contest for your viewers by means of CTA.

Tip #70 – Monitoring and Tracking

Most people who use YouTube didn't even know that this feature exists. YouTube has a very powerful analytics tool that provides insights about the videos being watched and the trend that is currently happening, you could use this to your advantage by analyzing what videos are being watched as well as the keywords being used to find them. This way, your video would be more effective in getting traffic, attention, and profit.

Conclusion

In conclusion, there are many benefits of utilizing social media as your marketing strategy for your business.

Listed below are some of the benefits which you can get if you make use of social media as one of your key online marketing strategies.

- ❖ Each and every social media platforms that we shared above has millions of users. If you follow the strategy properly, you will be able to reach out a big amount of targeted audiences easily. As you possibly notice, you may manage all of the social media platforms easily according to the 70 strategies above. You can use the content you have created on all of the social platforms easily.

- ❖ Social media marketing appears to be the most low cost marketing approach in business world. You need not to spend a big amount of money for this particular type of online marketing strategy. All of these social platforms are free of charge unless you wish to gain some extra features which are not necessary from the strategies that we shared above. All you have to do is create an account, build your profile and start posting photos, content and videos about your business. With this level of cost effectiveness, this medium is definitely hard to ignore. You can gain a lot even if you do not shell out that much money.

- ❖ In general, these types of websites are used by numerous individuals to socialize and interact with their friends. This is also one good way if you wish to meet new people whom you share the same interests with. With the level of personalization allowed on these sites, you can definitely use it to connect to your customers. In the long run, you may even ask for feedbacks, post surveys, answer questions asked by your existing and potential clients.

- ❖ Sharing is caring. You will also get to enjoy faster information dissemination. Since millions of users use social media every minute then you get be assured that any information that you wish to distribute or promote will reach as many as possible.

Thank you again for downloading this book!

I hope this book was able to help you to boost your business significantly.

If you enjoyed this book, please take the time to share your thoughts and post a review on Amazon. It'd be greatly appreciated!

If you wish to learn about another powerful marketing strategy for your business, please feel free to read my another top seller book:

A Proven, Step-By-Step Guide on How to Use Blog Marketing Strategy to Boost Your Business Significantly!

Blog Marketing Strategy

» Read more..

- ➢ The reasons why Blog Marketing can instantly boost up your Business.
- ➢ Step-by-step on choosing the best blogging platform for your business blog.
- ➢ Step-by-step on finding a money keyword with 4 criteria for keyword research.
- ➢ Step-by-step on what to blog and how to blog.
- ➢ Step-by-step on producing top notch contents for your blog.
- ➢ Step-by-step on promoting and generating traffic to your business blog.
- ➢ Step-by-step on integrating the powerful viral marketing for your business blog.
- ➢ Monitoring and tracking your business blog performance.
- ➢ Much, much more!

Download your copy today and start applying these business blogging tips to boost your business significantly!

BOOKS FROM POGO BOOK PUBLISHING

Business and Investing

1. Make Money Online – 7 Days to Build a Profitable Online Business

A Proven, Step-By-Step Guide to Start Making Money Online by Building a Profitable Online Business in 7 Days!

Now Everyone Can Make Money Online.
Continue reading →

2. Social Media Strategy – 70 Social Media Strategies to Boost your Business

Discover 70 Ways of Social Media Strategy to Boost Your Business Significantly!

You'll Create More Social Media Engagement, Attract More Customers And Sales by Following this Social Media Strategy Handbook

» Read more..

3. Blog Marketing – A Proven Blog Marketing Strategy to Boost Your Business Significantly

A Proven, Step-By-Step Guide on How to Use Blog Marketing Strategy to Boost Your Business Significantly!

Blog Marketing Strategy

» Read more..

Health and Fitness

1. Cancer Cure – When Chemotherapy is Not the Only Option for Cancer Cure

Is Chemotherapy the only Option for Cancer Cure?

Let me share a story first. A friend of mine found out that he has lung cancer. He went through the surgery and several rounds of chemotherapy. He was suffering and weak. After the treatment, the tumor has been successfully removed and cleared from his body. While he is so relieved and happy, the doctor told him that the cancer has relapsed with more aggressive. He went through another round of chemotherapy

2. Cancer Diet – A Complete Diet Plan for Cancer Prevention, Cancer Cure and Cancer Recovery

What Should We Eat for Cancer Prevention, Cancer Cure and Cancer Recovery?

Cancer is a class of diseases characterized by uncontrolled growth and spread of abnormal cells in the body. Cancer may affect anyone of us.

» Read more..

Disclaimer

This e-book has been written for information purposes only. Every effort has been made to make this ebook as complete and accurate as possible. However, there may be mistakes in typography or content. Also, this e-book provides information only up to the publishing date. Therefore, this ebook should be used as a guide - not as the ultimate source.

The purpose of this ebook is to educate. The author and the publisher does not warrant that the information contained in this e-book is fully complete and shall not be responsible for any errors or omissions. The author and publisher shall have neither liability nor responsibility to any person or entity with respect to any loss or damage caused or alleged to be caused directly or indirectly by this e-book.

About the Author

Lancaster Collins is a young professional internet entrepreneur. He started his business via internet and network marketing since 2006. He is earning 5 figures annually just from his part-time online business.

www.ingramcontent.com/pod-product-compliance
Lightning Source LLC
Chambersburg PA
CBHW070717180526
45167CB00004B/1515